CLASSIC CARS
WOODIES
A NATIONAL TREASURE

CLASSIC CARS
WOODIES
A NATIONAL TREASURE

BILL YENNE

FIRST GLANCE BOOKS
COBB, CALIFORNIA

Published by O.G. Publishing, Inc.

© 1997 O.G. Publishing, Inc.

Distributed by First Glance Books, Inc.
PO Box 960
Cobb, CA 95426
Phone: (707) 928-1994
Fax: (707) 928-1995

This edition was produced by
American Graphic Systems, Inc.
PO Box 460313
San Francisco, CA 94146

The author wishes to thank the following people for their generous assistance in this project: Marilyn Backus of Kughn Enterprises; Helen Earley of the Oldsmobile History Center; Jeanne Gilkey; Laura Mancini of GM Media Archives; Andi Welles and the Santa Cruz Woodies Chapter of the National Woodies Club: Dave Welles, president and Pat Benfield, secretary.

Text © 1997 Bill Yenne. Design © 1997 American Graphic Systems, Inc.

Designed and captioned by Bill Yenne, with design and research assistance from Azia Yenne.
Proofreading by Amy Bokser.

Each black & white photograph was supplied through the courtesy of the maker of the car represented in the photograph.

All color photographs are © 1997 Bill Yenne, with the following exceptions:
Author's collection: 6 (top); David Bolzano Hollywood Images: 10 (bottom); Ford Motor Company: 8 (bottom), 9 (top), 70 (bottom), 71 (bottom); Kughn Enterprises: 16 (bottom), 17 (bottom) 28-29 (all), 124 (bottom left), 139 (bottom right); Dan and Maureen Wiseman: 56-57 (all).

Page one photograph: A 1948 Chevrolet Fleetmaster and friends.
Photograph on preceding pages: A close-up view of a 1951 Ford Country Squire.
Photograph above: A detail view of a 1948 Ford Super DeLuxe Eight owned by Jeanne Gilkey.

ISBN 1-885440-06-5

Printed in Hong Kong

———

TABLE OF CONTENTS

✹

INTRODUCTION

✦

[Above: An 1860 Concord stagecoach.]

[Below: A 1920 Ford depot hack.]

[Opposite: A detail from a 1948 Chevrolet Fleetmaster.]

Woodies evoke a past era of magical summer days, outings in the country and surfin' safaris to sun-washed beaches. Woodies always turn heads, and, as woodie-owner Jeanne Gilkey has pointed out, the sight of a woodie almost always brings a smile.

The classic era of the American woodie lasted from the late 1930s through the early 1950s. During that period, Ford, Chrysler, and General Motors all produced variations on the theme. These became an integral part of the American lifestyle, first as a comfortable family car and then as the car of choice for surfers and beach-goers. Woodies have their roots in the classic coach-making tradition that extends back into the eighteenth century, and which flourished in the nineteenth century. The most famous of these vehicles were the "Concord" stagecoaches manufactured by Abbot-Downing in Concord, New Hampshire. These became a common sight in America, and an icon of the Old West.

Early in the twentieth century, as practical gasoline engines became available, it was natural that wood-framed, gasoline-powered motor vehicles – the forerunners of the classic woodies – began to appear. The first were "depot hacks" and delivery vehicles, but by 1910, there were "estate wagons" that were actually used by wealthy people to travel around their estates. In the beginning, these were

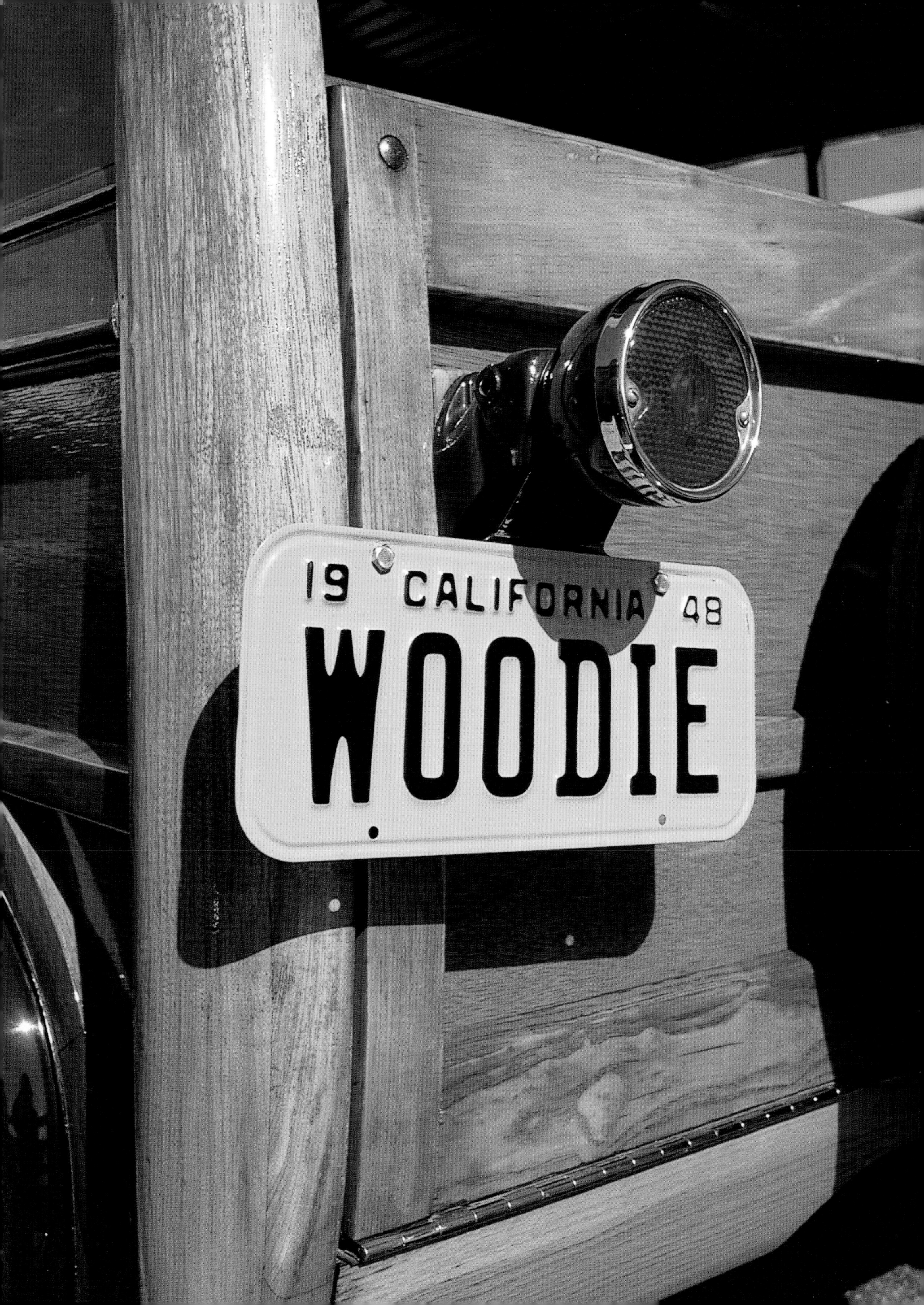
19 CALIFORNIA 48
WOODIE

manufactured by the former coach and wagon
makers. In the 1920s, as automobile companies
such as Ford, Willys and Dodge Brothers got
involved in building chassis and drive trains, the
wooden bodies continued to be made by firms
such as Martin-Parry, Mifflinburg and Wildanger,
who specialized in coach work.

By the 1930s, wood-framed and wood-pan-
eled automobiles became part of the standard
line of cars offered by all the major American
car-makers. Ford, Chrysler, and General Motors
routinely produced woodies through the 1930s
and 1940s. Most were station wagons, but there
were also notable convertibles by Mercury and
Chrysler, among others.

During those years, the Ford Motor Company produced more woodies than any other company, and actually opened its own wood mill at
Iron Mountain on Michigan's Upper Peninsula to

make the bodies. Iron Mountain was, incidentally, conveniently close to vast, Ford-owned, hardwood forests.

This book is a photo album of classic woodies, with examples of most of the important makes and model years. It is a celebration of great woodies, their classic era, and of the rapidly-growing woodie revival, which is putting more of these great machines on the street and in the public eye.

Woodies have been called *the collectors' car of the decade*, but they are really timeless. With their magnificent styling and lush wood detailing, they are not so much means of transportation as they are rolling works of art — indeed, rolling masterpieces.

1 9 4 7
B U I C K

✧

The January 1954 marriage of Joe DiMaggio and Marilyn Monroe united one of the greatest baseball legends with the sexy starlet who was then the reigning goddess of Hollywood. The couple eluded the press to escape to honeymoon on Catalina Island off the California coast. It was here that Philip Wrigley of the Wrigley chewing gum family lent them the use of his 1947 Buick Eight. The 298th of 300 such woodies, this car was purchased by John Fleming in 1973. It still has original paint and the original engine with 30,000 miles. The 1947 Buick Series 70 Roadmaster Model 79 wagon was powered by a 144-horsepower, 320.2 cubic inch straight eight-cylinder engine. It had an advertised list price of $3,249 new. These cars had a wheelbase of 129 inches and a basic curb weight of 4,445 pounds empty.

[*Below: Joe and Marilyn. Right and overleaf: The Honeymoon car.*]

1 9 4 9

B U I C K

The 1949 Buick Super woodie was a
stylish vehicle in which white ash
framed mahogany panels, providing a beautiful
contrast and texture. As in earlier woodies, the
ash was a structural component of the body. The
Dynaflow transmission increased torque by way
of a drive turbine that was made to rotate in an
oil bath by a crankshaft driven turbine. The
1949 Buick Series 50 Super Model 59
wagon was powered by a 115/120-horsepower,
248 cubic inch straight eight-cylinder engine.
It had an advertised list price of $3,178 new,
and 1,847 were sold although not all were
woodies. Woodie Estate Wagons did remain a
Super option through 1953. These cars had
a hefty wheelbase of 121 inches and a basic
curb weight of 4,100 pounds minus passengers and gas.

[Below and right: A 1949 Buick Super.]

1938/1949 BUICKS

For Buick, 1938 meant an improved, higher horsepower "Dynaflash" engine and a restyled grill featuring wider horizontal bars. The 1938 Buick Series 60 Century Model 38-61 touring sedan was powered by a 141-horsepower, 320.2 cubic inch straight eight-cylinder engine. It had an advertised list price of $1,297 new, and 12,673 were sold. These cars had a wheelbase of 126 inches and a basic curb weight of 3,780 pounds. By the 1949 model year, all vestiges of prewar styling had faded. The year was marked by a sleeker, streamlined, "aircraft-style" look for Buick from Harley Earl's design

[Left: The 19 49 Buick Model 59 Station Wagon.]

[Below: The 1949 Roadmaster Ionia 79 Super Estate Wagon.]

[Opposite: The 1938 Buick Century Station Wagon.]

team. It was also the first year that Buicks would feature the signature "VentiPorts" or "portholes" on the side. An idea conceived by designer Ned Nickles, they would be a key Buick design feature until 1963. Three holes denoted a Super or a Special, while four holes were the mark of the Roadmaster family. The 1949 Buick Series 70 Roadmaster Model 79 wagon seen here was powered by a 150-horsepower, 320.2 cubic inch straight eight engine. It had an advertised list price of $3,734 new, and 653 were sold. The Dynaflow transmission was standard.

1939/1941 CHEVROLETS

✷

Chevrolet styling for the prewar years was simple and utilitarian, but plenty of wood was used. The 85-horsepower engine, introduced in 1939, was a key feature. The 1939 Chevy JB Master 85 wagon was powered by an 85-horsepower, 216.5 cubic inch straight six-cylinder engine. It had an advertised list price of $848 and a basic curb weight of 3,010 pounds. The JA Master DeLuxe wagon was powered by the same six-cylinder engine. It had an adver-tised list price of $883 new, and weighed 3,060 pounds. Both the JA and the JB had a wheel-base of 112.3 inches. Chevrolet called the wagon seen below a "Truck Carry-all," although it was similar in styling to the 1941 AH Special DeLuxe wagon seen on the following pages. The engine, upgraded from 1939's 85 horses, was a 90-horsepower, 216.5 cubic inch straight six.

———————

[*Left: A 1939 Chevy Station Wagon. Below: A 1941 Wagon*]

1941
CHEVROLET

For the 1941 Chevrolet Special Deluxe, Harley Earl's designers pulled out all the stops to create styling that was quite advanced for the time, and which would survive, essentially unchanged, for the remainder of the war-interrupted decade. The 1941 Chevy AH Special DeLuxe wagon had an advertised list price of $995 new, and 2,045 were sold, including cabriolet convertible coupes as well as woodie wagons. The Special DeLuxes had a wheelbase of 116 inches and a basic curb weight of 3,410 pounds minus passengers and gas. The Special DeLuxes were powered by a 90-horsepower, 216.5 cubic inch straight six-cylinder engine. The increase in horsepower over the previously standard 85 was achieved with higher compression made possible by redesigned pistons, compression chambers, valves, and rockers.

[*Left and below: A 1941 Chevrolet Special DeLuxe woodie:*]

1 9 4 8

CHEVROLET

✳

The last model year that Chevrolet would produce a woodie wagon with true wood structural components was 1948. The crown jewel of the woodie fleet that year was the appropriately named Fleetmaster. The Fleetmaster, and the Stylemaster, were introduced in 1946, superceding the prewar Special DeLuxe Series. In 1948, as in 1946, the Fleetmaster wagon was powered by a 90-horsepower, 216.5 cubic inch straight six-cylinder engine. For the 1948 Fleetmaster, the advertised list price was $2,013 compared to $1,712 in 1946. But the United States was a awash in postwar prosperity by 1948, and growing families wanted wagons. In 1948, 10,171 were sold, compared to only 804 two years before. The 1948 Fleetmaster had a wheelbase of 116 inches and a basic curb weight of 3,465 pounds.

[Below, right and overleaf: A 1948 Chevrolet Fleetmaster.]

1945
CHRYSLER

✴

At the end of World War II, Chrysler expanded the Town & Country line — which had been limited to wagons before the war — with the the introduction of a sedan and convertible. Many more convertibles than hardtops were built in 1945. The company also spiffed up the Town & Country with a new "eggcrate" grille. The 1945 Chrysler C-38/39 Town & Country Hardtop Coupe was powered by a 135-horsepower, 323.5 cubic inch straight eight-cylinder engine. It was a prototype and only 7 were sold. These cars had a wheelbase of 121.5 inches. The 1945 Chrysler C-38/39 Town & Country convertible coupe was powered by a 135-horsepower, 323.5 cubic inch eight engine. It had an advertised list price of $2,743 new, and 1,935 were sold. These cars had a wheelbase of 121.5 inches and a basic curb weight of 4332 pounds.

[Below: The popular 1945 Chrysler Town & Country convertible.

Right: A 1945 Chrysler Town & Country hardtop.]

1947·1948 CHRYSLERS

✦

The 1947 Chrysler model year was marked by changes in detailing that would be retained in the nearly-identical 1948 models. In the Windsor Town & Country this included new wheels, hubcaps, choices of color, and fender trim. Also available were the Goodyear Super Cushion low-pressure tires. As can be seen in these fine machines from the Kughn Enterprises collection in Michigan, the glittering eggcrate grille of the 1945 Town & Country was retained. The 1946-1948 years were important for the Chrysler Town & Country for they represented the highest sales years ever

for that model, as well as the highest for any model that would be seen for some time. The 1947 Chrysler C-38/39 Town & Country convertible coupe was powered by a 135-horsepower, 323.5 cubic inch eight engine. It had a list price of $2,998. These cars had a wheelbase of 127.5 inches and a curb weight of 4,332 pounds. The 1948 Chrysler C-38W Windsor sedan was powered by a 114-horsepower, 250.6 cubic inch six engine. It had a list price of $2,021 new. These cars had a wheelbase of 121.5 inches and weighed 3,528 pounds.

1948
CHRYSLER (I)

The 1948 Chrysler Town & Country convertible woodie is clearly one of the most prized and most "head-turning" vehicles in woodidom. Of these, perhaps the most famous is that which was owned by the film star Leo Carrillo. With its full steer head (not just the horns, mind you) it turns the most heads. A popular leading man, Carrillo was acclaimed in such films as *Love Me Forever* (1935), *History is Made at Night* (1937), *American Empire* (1942) and *The Fugitive* (1947). Though most of his films were not Westerns, he cultivated a Western persona and is best known for starring as "Pancho" in the 1950s television series *The Cisco Kid*. In 1948, he bought this splendid convertible, which was later part of Bill Harrah's automobile collection before being acquired by the Imperial Palace in Las Vegas.

[Left and below: Leo Carrillo's steer-headed 1948 woodie.]

1948
CHRYSLER (II)

✳

The 1948 Town & Country convertible was perhaps the most memorable of Chrysler's wonderful woodies. The 1948 Chrysler C-38/39 Town & Country convertible coupe was powered by a 135-horsepower, 323.5 cubic inch Spitfire straight-8 engine and featured the trademarked Fluid Drive transmission. It had an advertised list price of $3,420 new, and 3,309 were sold. These cars had a wheelbase of 127.5 inches and a basic curb weight of 4,332 pounds minus passengers and gas.

[Above and opposite: Chrome and mahogany styling in the 1948 Town & Country.]

[Below: Cruising in a 1948 Town & Country convertible.]

[Overleaf: Chrome and mirrors reflect a Town & Country's ash and mahogany.]

1936
DODGE

✹

One can generally expect to find woodies at the beach, so the use of a woodie as an official lifeguard vehicle should come as no surprise. However, owner Dick DeLuna has marked the rear of his 1936 Westchester Suburban "For Unofficial Use Only." Can a surfing safari to California's Seabright Beach be considered "unofficial?" Named for the posh suburban county immediately north of New York City, the 1936 Westchester Suburban wagon was powered by an 87 horsepower, 217.8 cubic inch straight-six engine. The styling included maple paneling, a much lighter wood than the mahogany favored by other carmakers. Based on a Dodge light truck chassis, the Westchester had a wheelbase of 116 inches and was built solidly for heavy work — including the carrying of surfboards — and up to eight passengers.

[Left and below: Dick DeLuna's 1936 Dodge.]

1949
DODGE

✦

The 1949 model year was marked by the first major redesign in body styling that had been seen at Dodge since before World War II. Separate front fenders were gone forever and a bold new grille with wide bars was introduced. Unlike General Motors, who was phasing out woodies in 1949, Dodge kept woodies in the line-up against the backdrop of this restyling. The mahogany that was used for the paneling was trimmed with lighter and contrasting ash, a typical format for woodies produced in the late 1940s. The 1949 Dodge D-30 Coronet wagon was powered by a 103-horsepower, 230.2 cubic inch six-cylinder engine. It had an advertised list price of $2,865 new, and 800 were sold. These cars had a wheelbase of 123.5 inches and a basic curb weight of 3,830 pounds minus passengers and gas.

[*Below and right: Roland Baker's 1949 Dodge.*]

1929
FORD

Ford introduced the Model A in 1928 after building 15 million virtually identical Model Ts over a period of 19 years. Henry Ford had used mass production to become the leading car-maker in the world. However, during the roaring twenties, styling was becoming more important. While companies such as Chevrolet introduced new models periodically, Fords were repetitive for those 19 years. The Model A was designed to change that, and 1929 saw the debut of the birch- or maple-paneled Model A woodie. However, the use of wood was a tradition that dated back to Ford's earlier depot hacks and other delivery vehicles. The one pictured here has been heavily modified, and the radiator cap is clearly not stock. This color would not have met with Henry Ford's taste for "any color, so long as it is black."

[Left and below: A modified 1929 Model A Ford woodie:]

1930 FORD

During the 1930 model year, Ford introduced a number of styling changes in the Model A that had been conceived by Edsel Ford, the son of the founder. The crest of the hood was moved up, while the fenders were moved down and made wider. Stainless steel replaced nickel-plated steel in the radiator and headlight housings, and of course, there was a woodie wagon among the spectrum of style choices. The 1930 Ford Model A wagon was powered by a 40-horsepower, 200.5 cubic inch inline four-cylinder engine. It had a list price of $640 new, and 3,790 were sold. These cars had a wheelbase of 103.5 inches. In 1931, the Model A wagon would be nearly identical, with the price down slightly with the onset of the Depression. While 3,018 were sold in 1931, the Depression forced production to a mere 1,400 in 1932.

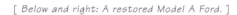

[*Below and right: A restored Model A Ford.*]

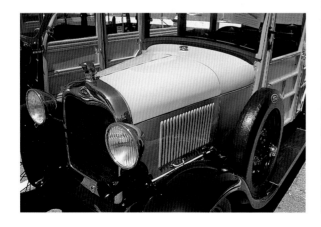

1 9 3 3 · 1 9 3 7
F O R D *s*

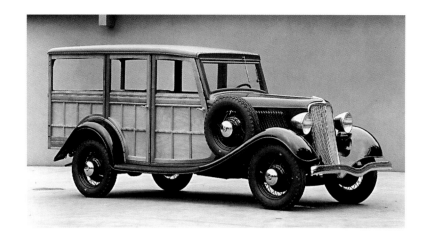

Ford wagons for 1933 introduced a much more fluid, streamlined look that would characterize these vehicles through 1937. The 1933 Ford wagons were powered by a 50-horsepower, 200.5 cubic inch inline four cylinder engine, or a 221 cubic inch, 75-horsepower V8. The average list price was $615. In 1937, wagons had a choice of a 136 cubic inch, 60 horsepower V8 engine or a 221 cubic inch, 85 horsepower V8. The average sticker price was $759. All these cars had a 112 inch wheelbase.

[*Above: The 1933 Ford Model 46 station wagon.*]

[*Below and Opposite: The spacious 1937 Ford station wagons offered a choice of glass side windows or the traditional coach-style curtains.*]

1 9 3 5
F O R D

While the 112-inch chassis would remain in use for another five years, 1935 saw a major styling change for Ford — the introduction of a much more angular grill — which would be present for more than a decade. For station wagons, the company reached another important milestone. The 1935 model year marked the beginning of Ford's building the wooden bodies for the wagons at its own Iron Mountain plant, which was located amid the hardwood forests of Michigan's Upper Peninsula. Prior to 1935, the bodies had been built in Detroit by Murray & Briggs, using Kentucky birch and maple. The 1935 Ford Model 48 woodie wagon was powered by a 90-horsepower, 221 cubic inch V8 engine. It had an advertised list price of $670 new, and 4,536 of these stylish woodies were sold.

[Below and right: A 1935 Model 48 woodie station wagon.]

1938
FORD

✦

The Model 81A Ford DeLuxe for 1938 offered a redesigned grille and glass windows, whereas the 1937 Ford Model 74 wagon had the option of either glass side windows or curtains. The 1938 Model 82A Standards used 1937 bodies. The Model 81A was powered by an 85-horsepower, 221 cubic inch V8 engine. It had an advertised list price of $825 new, and 6,944 were sold. All 1937 and 1938 models had a wheelbase of 112 inches and the 81A's basic curb weight was 2,981 pounds.

[Above: Harry and Phoebe Linden's bird's eye maple 1938 DeLuxe.]

[Below and opposite: Dave and Andi Welles' 1938 Ford Model 81A.]

1939
FORD

Redesigning and cleaning up the fender line to completely blend in the headlights was a styling feature developed for the 1939 Ford DeLuxe by Bob Gregorie and Edsel Ford. Meanwhile, one step behind, the 1939 Model 92A Standard, meanwhile, revisited the body styling of the 1938 DeLuxe. The 1939 models also marked the year that Ford would follow other car-makers by finally adopting hydraulic, rather than mechanical, brakes. As with similar models for the preceding two years, the 1939 Model 91A DeLuxe was powered by an 85-horsepower, 221 cubic inch V8 engine. The sticker price climbed to $840, and 6,155 (slightly fewer than in 1938) were sold. The 112-inch wheelbase chassis was retained, and the Model 81A had a basic curb weight of 2,981 pounds minus passengers and gas.

[Below and right: Jim and Pam Colores' 1939 Ford DeLuxe.]

1 9 4 0

FORD (I)

For 1940, Bob Gregorie redesigned the Ford DeLuxe nose and grille, taking advantage of sealed-beam headlights which fit into, and became part of, the fender. The grille became more delicate, but it was "echoed" by small demi-grilles situated on a "catwalk" ridge that separated the fender from the body on either side. The 1940 Ford 01A V8/85 DeLuxe wagon was powered by an 85-horsepower, 221 cubic inch V8 engine. It had an advertised list price of $947 new, and 8,730 were sold. While Chevrolet had eclipsed Ford as America's foremost carmaker by 1940, Ford wagons outsold Chevy's Special DeLuxe wagons by better than three to one. The 1940 Ford 01A V8/85 had a wheelbase of 112 inches and a basic curb weight of 3,262 pounds.

[Below and right: A 1940 Ford DeLuxe woodie wagon.]

[Overleaf: The subtle bird's eye maple of a 1940 Ford.]

1940 FORD RESTORATION

✦

Building a woodie was once a relatively routine affair. There was a span of more than a dozen years during which they literally rolled off assembly lines in and around Detroit. But those days are long gone, never again to be revisited. Today, *maintaining a woodie in some semblance of the original condition is a matter of constant attention to maintenance and care of the wood, while the process of getting a woodie into shape may actually involve a restoration process that comes close to building the car from scratch.* Such was the three-year odyssey undertaken by Dan and Maureen Wiseman of San Martin, California. Through the entire process of bringing their 1940 Special back to life, they never lost sight of the fact that it was once a tree.

[*Above: The original wood required complete replacement.*]

[*Below: Dan was pleased to see it finally coming together.*]

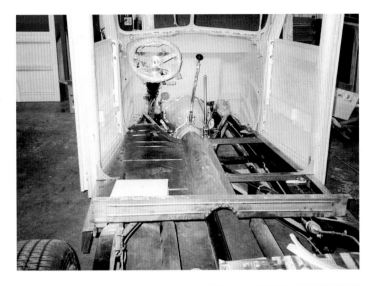

[Above: The maple came from Cincinnati Woodworks, and the assembly work took place at Michael J's in San Jose, California.]

[Below and overleaf: The Wiseman's DeLuxe restored to a glory it hadn't seen in half a century – with a 350HO, 345-horsepower Chevy engine.]

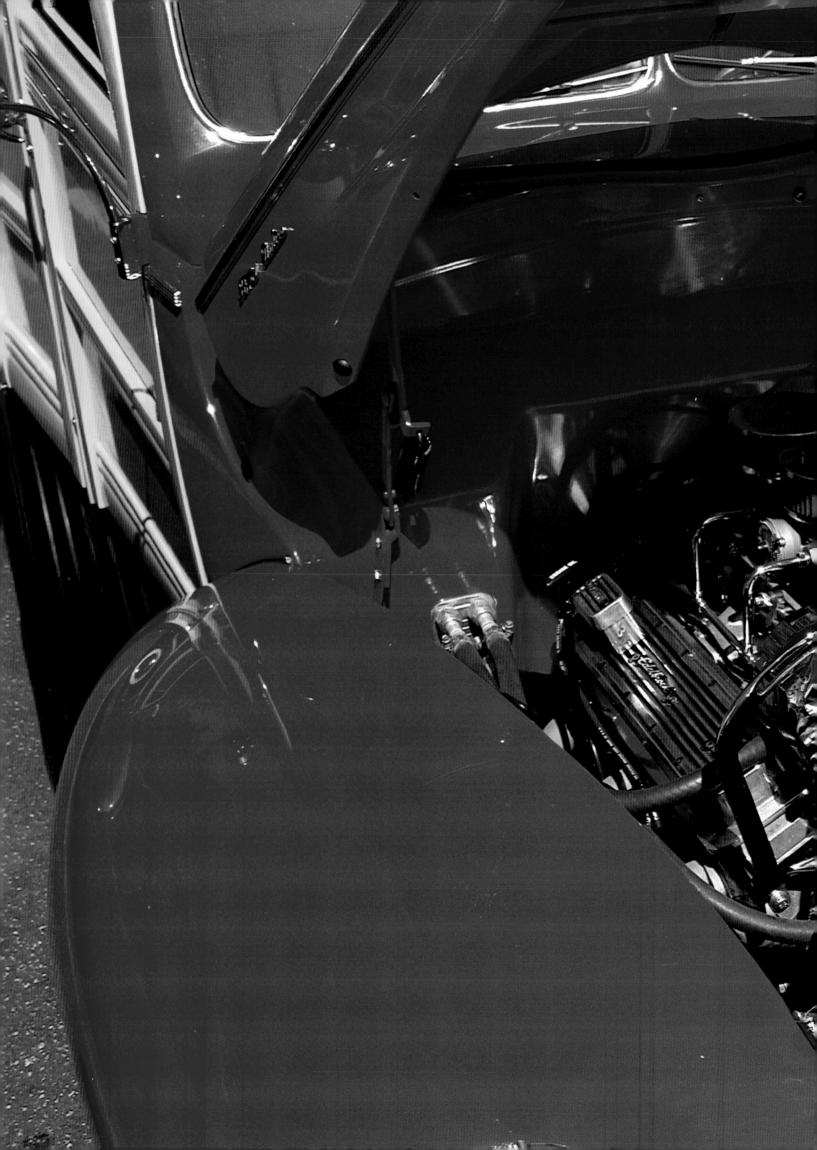

1940 FORD (II)

✦

In the folklore of car culture – whether the cars are stock, custom, modified, or antique – there are numerous tales of painstaking (and often painful) restoration project to return well-worn woodies to mint or better condition. In the case of Howard Benfield's 1940 Ford woodie, the tale is different, but just as complex. It was 1964, and Howard was living another woodie tradition, that of the high school kid keen on longboard surfing. The images of surfing and woodies meshed in the 1960s when surfers bought woodies because they were still cheap and readily available. Howard bought his woodie from an old fisherman in Santa Cruz, California and went surfing. Over the ensuing decades, he deliberately preserved the car in the same condition it was when he acquired it on that summer day so long ago.

[*Below and right: Howard Benfield's 1940 woodie.*]

1941·1942 FORDS

The 1941 Fords were the largest and heaviest that the carmaker had yet produced, with the wheelbase expanded to 114 inches, and the grille — now actually three grilles — greatly expanded. In 1942, the grilles would blend as one in a preview of postwar styling. The 1941 Ford 1GA Six Super DeLuxe wagon was powered by a 90-horsepower, 226 cubic inch straight six cylinder engine. It had an advertised list price of $998 new. These cars had a basic curb weight of 3,400 pounds minus passengers and gas. The 1942 woodie was available as a 21A V8 Super DeLuxe wagon powered by a 90-horsepower, 221 cubic inch V8 engine, or a 90-horsepower straight-six. They had sticker prices of $1,125 and $1,115 respectively, and 5,482 were sold before World War II halted production for the next four years.

[Left A 1941 Super DeLuxe. Below: A 1942 Model 21A.]

1946
FORD (1)

✺

Having built jeeps and B-24 bombers during World War II, Ford quickly returned to car-making for the peacetime 1946 model year. The design was similar to the 1942, but the grille was now composed of bold bars instead of delicate splines. The 1946 Ford 6GA Six Super DeLuxe Model 79B wagon was powered by a 90-horsepower, 226 cubic inch straight six cylinder engine. It had an advertised list price of $1,504 new. These cars had a wheelbase of 114 inches and weighed 3,457 pounds.

[Above: A 1946 Ford ready for a surfing safari.]

[Below, opposite and overleaf: Jim Vickery's 1946 Ford woodie wagon.]

1946
FORD (II)

✦

A great deal has been written through the years about Santa Claus. Clement Moore vividly described the sleigh he drives annually on December 25, but what ride conveys him the rest of the year? What else but a tastefully maintained maroon 1946 Ford Super DeLuxe woodie wagon? The only question that remains is to ask whether — if you're not naughty, but nice — you'll catch a glimpse this year of his jolliness in his woodie wagon. To this, the answer is a cryptic "Knock on wood."

[Above: The lush paneling of a 1946 Super DeLuxe.]

[Below and opposite: The 1946 woodie of Steve McCormick, aka S.Claus.]

1946
FORD (III)

✸

Postwar optimism and the pent-up
demand for new consumer goods
played a role in Ford's development of the 1946
69A V8 Super DeLuxe Sportsman convertible
Model 71. Bob Gregorie had designed the new
convertible during the war, while Willys jeeps were
rolling down the Ford assembly line and workers
everywhere were dreaming of a spin down the
highway in a new car. For his new woodie convertible, Gregorie chose the mahogany paneling
trimmed in white ash that had characterized his
woodie wagons since the prewar shift from solid
maple. The wood was simply trim, however, and

[Left: A drive in the country in the 1946 Sportsman.]

[Below: An interior detail view of the Sportsman.]

[Opposite: The Sportsman reminded some people of

Chrysler's Town & Country convertible coupe.]

not structural as in the wagons. The interior was leather, of course. The name "Sportsman" was coined to inspire thoughts of breezy weekend getaways with a duck gun or a picnic hamper filled with the goodies long-forbidden by wartime rationing. The Sportsman convertible Model 71 was powered by a 100-horsepower, 239.4 cubic inch V8 engine. It had an advertised list price of $1,982 new, and 1,209 were sold. These cars had the now-standard wheelbase of 114 inches and a basic curb weight of 3,340 pounds minus passengers and gas.

1 9 4 7

F O R D

✵

The 1947 model year reflected less of a change in styling than had been seen in Fords since the Model A. In terms of styling — if not price and powerplant — the 1947 7GA Six and 79A V8 Super DeLuxes wagons were essentially the same as the 1946 6GA and 69A V8. In terms of engine specifications, the 7GA Six Super DeLuxe wagon was powered by a 90-horsepower, 226 cubic inch straight six cylinder engine, while the 79A V8 Super DeLuxe wagon was powered by a 100-horsepower, 239.4 cubic inch V-8. The advertised list prices of the two vehicles were of $1,893 and $1,972 respectively. Both had the standard Ford wheelbase of 114 inches, and their basic curb weights were 3,487 pounds and 3,520 pounds respectively.

[Left: A 1947 Ford wagon with surfboard mirror.]

[Below and overleaf: Detailing on the 1947 Super Deluxe.]

1 9 4 8
F O R D   (I)

❂

Among woodie owners, certain icons always seem to prevail — Surfboards, dreams of Hawaii and wood's old nemesis: Woody Woodpecker. Woodie owners love Woody mostly for his pun value. The 1948 Ford 87HA Six Super DeLuxe Model 79B wagon was powered by a 95-horsepower, 226 cubic inch straight six cylinder engine. It had an advertised list price of $1,893 new. These cars had the Ford standard 114-inch wheelbase and a basic curb weight of 3,487 pounds.

[These pages: A lemonade-yellow 1948 Super DeLuxe.]

[Overleaf: The beautiful lines of classic 1948 styling.]

1948
FORD (II)

✦

For Ford, the 1948 model year rounded out a three-year span in which styling remained virtually unchanged, albeit magnificent. Three years of the same design insured that a single style would outnumber any other model from any other maker and create a definitive woodie "look." These vehicles are true classics, with just the right mix of wood, chrome, and bold, confident colors. In short, they don't make 'em like this anymore. Wherever woodies gather, the 1946-1948 Ford Super DeLuxe will be there.

[These pages: This 1948 Super DeLuxe is the pride and joy of engineering professor Jeanne Gilkey. Her other car is a 1979 Corvette.]

1949
FORD

✵

fter years with little or no change in styling, Ford undertook a radical redesign for 1949 which eliminated forever all vestiges of the prewar look. Several design teams worked independently on the project. These included Bob Gregorie's in-house group as well as several on the outside, including one headed by George Walker. As part of his effort, Walker hired Richard Caleal, late of General Motors, where he'd worked under Raymond Loewy. It was Caleal's design that fired the imagination of corporate management and became the image of 1949 for Ford. The 1949 Ford Custom V8 Model 79 wagon was powered by a 100-horse-power, 239.4 cubic inch V8 engine. It had an advertised list price of $2,119 new, and 31,412 were sold. These cars had a wheelbase of 114 inches and a basic curb weight of 3,543 pounds.

[Below and right: A 1949 two-door Model 79 wagon.]

1950
FORD (I)

The 1949 model year had seen the biggest changes in Ford styling since the Model A, and these changes were, not surprisingly, plagued with bugs. These were ironed out in the 1950 models, which retained the same Richard Caleal styling of 1949. As in 1949, Ford offered a two-door woodie wagon — known as the "Country Squire"— rather than the four-door configuration which had characterized the Super DeLuxe wagons of previous years. In retrospect, this was a curious choice, given that the Country Squire was billed as an "eight-passenger" vehicle. Also, station wagons were traditionally family cars, and access to the back seat is more difficult with a two-door. Possibly the choice was made to imbue the Squire with an aura of sportiness, or simply to make it easier to control the kids.

[*Below, right and overleaf: The 1950 Country Squire.*]

1 9 5 0
F O R D (II)

✺

With the 1950 Custom Country Squire, Ford began to offer the palette of color choices that would be identified so closely with the "fifties look" in automobiles. Red and blue had been around for years, but new colors such as turquoise and coral pink combined with Richard Caleal's all-new styling to make the new Fords appear truly of a different era. Ford also offered an engine choice in the Custom Country Squire Model C79 wagon. The options were the 226 cubic inch, 95-horsepower straight six-cylinder engine or the 239.4 cubic inch, 100 horsepower V-8. The Country Squire had a wheelbase of 114 inches and a basic curb weight of 3,511 pounds. The C79 had an advertised list price of $2,028 new, and 22,929 were sold — an amazing total when compared to the sales of prewar wagons, which never topped 10,000.

———————————

[These pages and overleaf: A coral pink 1950 C79.]

1951 FORD (I)

✸

A facelift was in the cards for Fords in the 1951 model year, as the single-bullet grille was replaced by a pair of smaller bullets positioned on the heavy horizontal bar. The 1951 Ford Custom Country Squire Model 79 wagon offered two engine options, the 95-horsepower option, 226 cubic inch straight-six cylinder motor; or the 100-horsepower 239.4 cubic inch V8. The Squire had an advertised list price of $2,029 – almost the same as 1950 – and 29,017 were sold – more than in 1950. The new cars retained a wheelbase of 114 inches and had a basic curb weight of 3,530 pounds. It was in the 1951 models that Ford would offer its first automatic transmission. Known as Ford-O-Matic Drive, it was a two-speed system similar to the Powerglide system which had been introduced by Chevrolet in 1950.

[*These pages and overleaf: Views of the 1951 wagon.*]

1951
FORD (II)

✪

Though future attempts would be made to recreate the look and feel of woodies 1951 would mark the final year that Ford would build a true wood-framed woodie. The 1951 Ford Custom Country Squire Model 79 wagon was the end of an era. Woodie wagons had been part of the line-up annually since before the Model A, but as early as 1952, the Country Squire would not only abandon structural wood, but the "look" of wood would be accomplished with plastic and decals, rather than real wood.

[*Above: The last Ford woodie sits for its official company portrait.*]

[*Below and opposite: A visor-equipped 1951 Country Squire.*]

1 9 4 6

M E R C U R Y

✦

Edsel Ford had created Mercury in 1939 as a slightly larger, slightly more elegant stablemate for Ford. In its early years, Mercury's styling generally paralleled that of its older sibling. In 1946, Mercurys still resembled Fords, but Mercury's postwar line-up included the all-new and very stylish Series 69M convertible coupe. Within the series were the Model 71 Sportsman and the Model 76, both powered by a 100-horsepower, 239.4 cubic inch V8 engine. The Model 71 had an advertised list price of $2,209, and the 76 was priced at $1,711. Sales of the two types were 205 and 6,044 respectively. Both vehicles had a wheelbase of 118 inches, four inches larger than contemporary Fords. and basic curb weights were 3,407 pounds minus passengers and gas for the Sportsman, and 3,340 pounds for the regular coupe.

[*Left and below: The 1946 Series 9M Sportsman.*]

1946 MARMON- HERRINGTON

One of the most unusual 1946 Mercurys still extant is the Marmon-Herrington All-Wheel Drive conversion. One of only four Mercury wagons built with a Ford truck four-speed drive train, this vehicle included Marmon-Herrington constant-velocity front hubs adapted to a 1939 differential, as well as Marmon-Herrington braking plates, brakes, and elliptical front parallel leaf springs. In 1948, noted ornithologist and photographer Don Bleitz had his car customized for camping by Coachcraft in Hollywood. This included a stainless steel ice chest and water tank built into the floor, with running water available at the dash board. Bleitz used it for his back country expeditions, which were featured in *Motor Trend* for October 1952, under the heading "Unique Cars for Sportsmen."

[*Below and right: Don Bleitz's unique 1946 Mercury.*]

1947·1948 MERCURYS

✴

Both Ford and Mercury retained their 1947 model year styling until the advent of the 1949 models. Indeed, the 1947-1948 grille was virtually identical to the 1946. This certainly made things go smoothly on the production line, but ironically, Mercury ran into production bugs with the woodies because the stock fenders wouldn't fit with the structural wood components and required modification. The 1947 and 1948 varied only in series number and in the number that were produced. The Mercury Series 79M(1947) and Series 89M(1948) Model 79 wagons were powered by 100-horsepower, 239.4 cubic inch V8 engines. For both years they had advertised list prices of $2,207, and 3,558 were sold in 1947, while 1,889 were sold in 1948. These cars had a wheelbase of 118 inches and a basic curb weight of 3,571 pounds.

[*Below and right: Styling for 1947-1948 was uniform.*]

1 9 4 8
M E R C U R Y

✹

The 1948 Mercury Series 89M woodies differed from the Model 79 wagons only in model number and serial number. The vehicle pictured here is an 89M from 1948 that is owned by Brent and Tobi Allred and has been restored with an "all-red" theme right down to the Allred's personalized plate: "REDWOOD." Although it is certainly an attractive material with many important applications, actual redwood was never used in woodies because it is among the softest of indigenous North American woods. For its postwar woodies, Mercury used mahogany for the dark paneling, framing it in maple or yellow birch. The finish was traditionally varnish, although current restoration projects will often employ the harder polyurethane finishes that were not available in the late 1940s during the halcyon days of American woodie production.

[*Below and right: Two view of the Allreds' REDWOOD.*]

1949 MERCURY (I)

✧

When World War II ended, both Ford and Mercury revisited their 1942 styling as a inspiration for their 1946 models, and then appeared to give their stylists a three year vacation. However, something was cooking with the styling chefs during that time, and the result was a bold new look in 1949 for both Dearborn firms. Both companies retained their basic chassis — Ford with a 114 inch wheelbase, and Mercury with 118 inches — but everything else changed. They were lower, and hence they appeared wider. Despite their apparent bulkiness, the new Mercurys looked sleek, streamlined and aerodynamically clean. The 1949 Mercury Series 9CM Model 79 wagon and the Model 72 coupe were powered by a 110-horsepower, 255.4 cubic inch V8 engine. The wagon had an advertised list price of $2,716 new and 8,044 were sold, while the coupe had a list price of $1,979 and 120,616 were sold. The wagon had a basic curb weight of 3,626 pounds minus passengers and gas, whereas the coupe had a basic curb weight of 3,321 pounds. Less structural wood was used for the new 1949s than had been present previously.

[Right: The aerodynamic Mercury 9CM for 1949.]

[Overleaf: A detail from Brent and Tobi Allred's REDWOOD.]

1 9 5 0
M E R C U R Y

Mercury models for 1950 retained the revolutionary styling that had been introduced in 1949, and they retained the 118-inch wheelbase that dated from before the second World War. The 1950 Mercury Series 0CM Model M-79 wagon was powered by a 110-horse-power, 255.4 cubic inch V8 engine. It had an advertised list price of $2,561 new, and just 1,746 were sold. These cars had a basic curb weight of 3,755 pounds. The Mercury publicity photograph at the right captures the image of the Mercury owners as the Mercury imagined them. A fashionable youngish couple is setting out on a trip to the country, possibly to a vacation cabin. They are more upwardly-mobile than an average Ford family, but not quite as well heeled as the demographic that Ford imagined for its top-of-the-line Lincolns.

[*Below and right: The 1950 Mercury wagon.*]

1 9 4 9
M E R C U R Y   (I I)

Historically, the 1949 Mercury was designed for a specific niche. The Mercury itself was developed for an upscale growing middle class whose parents drove Fords and who would themselves one day graduate to Lincolns. As for the 1949 model, it was a harbinger on the threshold of that brave new world of prosperity and forward-looking style that would be the 1950s. By the 1960s, the ebullient enthusiasm had faded, and the harbinger of a glamorous age had gone surfing.

[These pages: Always a classic, the 1949 Mercury 9CM wagon.]

1952

MERCURY

By the early 1950s, the use of structural wood in station wagon construction was largely a thing of the past, and the era of decals and fiberglass trim was just around the corner. For Mercury, who had produced some magnificent woodies a scant few years before, the transition was subtle, with a growing number of station wagons being built without wood, and the woodies themselves having less and less wood each year. For the 1952 model year — as the "fins" that would define the cars of the later 1950s had begun to emerge from the rear fenders — the mahogany panels

were gone, replaced by plastic, and only the light wood framing remained. Soon that too, would be little more than a memory. The two 1952 Mercury wagons were the Series 2M Model 79B wagon, which carried six people and the Model 79D wagon, which carried eight. They were priced at $2,525 and $2,570 respectively, and were each powered by a 125-horsepower, 255.4 cubic inch V8 engine. They had the long-standard 118-inch Mercury wheelbase and a basic curb weight of 3,800 pounds minus passengers and gas. Between the 79B and 79D, 2,487 were sold.

1940

OLDSMOBILE

(I)

✳

The 1940 Oldsmobile F-40 Series 60 wagon was a limited edition vehicle, with only 633 built. By the 1990s, only three were known to still be in existence, including the one pictured here, which is owned by Barbara Giosso. The original list price was $1,042, and the three survivors have clearly appreciated many times over. The Series 60 wagon was a beautiful machine, with its structural wood body and wider grille and fenders than Oldsmobile had used in its cars during the 1930s. It was powered by a 95-horsepower, 229.7 cubic inch straight six-cylinder engine. It was the first Oldsmobile wagon to have the generous 116 inch wheelbase and it had a basic curb weight of 3,255 pounds minus passengers and gas.

[Below and right: Barbara Giosso's 1940 Olds.]

1940
OLDSMOBILE
(II)

✦

Oldsmobile clearly considered demo-graphics and lifestyle in the cre-ation of the 1940 F-40 Series 60 wagon. It was a perfect second car when friends and family were taking weekend trips to the country home, or simply driving up for a day on the polo field. With comfortable interior and its great capacity for luggage, the Series 60 was also ideal for long car trips.

[Above: A Series 60 detail view.]

[Below and opposite: Oldsmobile's view of the ideal Series 60 families.]

1941
OLDSMOBILE

✺

A word that could be used to describe Oldsmobile styling for 1941 would be "expansive." The impression was that everything was bolder and broader. The new grille was wider and heavier in appearance, and inside, a V8 powerplant was offered in the wagon for the first time, although woodie production was still very limited. Only 699 were made. The 1941 Oldsmobile 66 Special 6 wagon was powered by a 100-horsepower, 238.1 cubic inch straight six-cylinder engine. It had an advertised list price of $1,176 new, and 604 were sold. The 68 Special 8 wagon was powered by a 110-horsepower, 257.1 cubic inch V-8. It had a sticker price of $1,217, and just 95 were made. Both of the 1941 Olds wagons had a wheelbase of 119 inches and the basic curb weights were 3,565 pounds and 3,660 pounds respectively.

———

[*Left and below: The Oldsmobile 66 Special 6 for 1941.*]

1946
OLDSMOBILE

✦

During World War II, machine guns and aircraft engines took the place of 1943-1945 models on the Oldsmobiles assembly lines, as "Vs for Victory" and flags of Allied nations lent a patriotic atmosphere to the General Motors lobby. When victory had finally been achieved, thoughts turned back to consumer goods and to getting a 1946 model on the road as soon as possible. For most car-makers this meant revisiting the 1941-1942 styling, and Olds was no exception, although a new grille was included and more cars were built with the new HydraMatic transmission. The 1946 F-46 Special 66 wagon was powered by a 100-horsepower, 238.1 cubic inch straight six-cylinder engine. It had an advertised list price of $2,089 new, and only 140 were sold. It had a wheelbase of 119 inches and a basic curb weight of 3,750 pounds.

[*Left and below: The rare 1946 Oldsmobile F-46.*]

1947
OLDSMOBILE

✦

For the 1947 model year, Oldsmobile styling saw few changes. The division retained the grille that had been designed for the 1946 model, but enlarged the fender moldings. The HydraMatic transmission — which was introduced in 1939, but which had not been widely used until 1946 — continued to grow in popularity with the 1947 models. Oldsmobile continued to produce fewer woodie wagons than any other major car-maker, but they were offered in both six and eight cylinder configurations. The rare woodies numbered 968 in the six-cylinder form, and just 492 with the eight-cylinder

engine. The 1947 Oldsmobile F-47 Special 66 wagon was powered by a 100-horsepower, 238.1 cubic inch straight six-cylinder engine. It had an advertised list price of $2,456, and a basic curb weight of 3,770 pounds minus passengers and gas. The 1947 Oldsmobile E-47 Special 68 was powered by a 110-horsepower, 257.1 cubic inch straight eight-cylinder engine. The E-47 Special 68 had an advertised list price of $1,830 new, and a basic curb weight of 3,705 pounds minus passengers and gas. Both woodies had the Oldsmobile standard 119 inch wheelbase.

1948 OLDSMOBILE

✦

Oldsmobiles for 1948 were called "Dynamic," with a much more massive grille than the earlier postwar models, and with redesigned rear fenders which styling chief Harley Earl modeled after the tail fins of the Lockheed P-38 fighter aircraft. The effect of these fenders was fine on the sedan because they flowed back above the trunk line,. but on the woodie wagon, the rear was longer than the fenders. This was okay, because aircraft styling would have clashed with the whole idea of a woodie anyway. The 1948 Oldsmobile Dynamic 66 (or 68) wagon was powered by a 100- (or 110-) horsepower, 238.1 (or 257.1) cubic inch straight six-cylinder (or straight eight) engine. It had an advertised list price of $2,614 (or $2,672) new, and 840 (or 760) were sold. These cars had a basic curb weight of 3,620 (or 3,770) pounds.

[Left and below: Enjoying the Olds woodie for 1948.]

1 9 4 9
OLDSMOBILE

✴

The word "Futuramic" entered the Oldsmobile lexicon midway through the 1948 model year and served to define the division's styling image in 1949. In the case of sedans, Oldsmobile stylists had seen the future and the future said "fins." In the case of woodies, the future simply said "less wood." Wood remained only to frame the windows and in the form of a little strip of paneling that was used as a color accent the way a strip of chrome might be used. Indeed, with the joyous embrace of the wonders of modern technology, gleaming chrome summarized 1950s style far better than

wood, and this fact was not lost on American car-makers. Ironically, the 1949 woodies outsold any previous Olds woodies. The 1949 Oldsmobile Futuramic 76 wagon was powered by a 105-horsepower, 257.1 cubic inch straight six-cylinder engine. It had an advertised list price of $2,895 and 1,545 were produced. The Futuramic 76 had a basic curb weight of 3,770 pounds minus passengers and gas. The Futuramic 88 was powered by a 135-horsepower, 303.1 cubic inch V-8. It had a sticker price of $3,296 and a basic curb weight of 3,945 pounds.

1941
PACKARD (I)

Now just a quaint and distant memory, the Packard Motor Company was once the last word in style and excellence, and perhaps even in technical proficiency. Packards were the cars about which people dreamed. Today, Packard woodies are among the most highly prized. For 1941, Packard designed its body style with larger windows. The classic 1901 One Twenty Model 1493 wagon for 1941 was powered by a 120-horsepower, 282 cubic inch eight-cylinder engine. It had an advertised list price of $1,466 new. It had a standard, albeit ample, Packard wheelbase of 127 inches and a basic curb weight of 3,720 pounds.

[Left, below and overleaf: Packard's One Twenty for 1941.]

1 9 4 1
PACKARD (II)

✦

From the 1920s until the 1940s, Packard was one of the premier car-makers in the world, not only in terms of prestige, but in terms of production values as well. An important feature for 1941 was the Electromatic clutch, a manifold-vacuum operated fore-runner of the true automatic transmission, which permitted clutch-less shifting in and above second gear. The 1941 Packard One Ten wagon was powered by a 130-horsepower, 288 cubic inch straight eight-cylinder engine. It had an advertised list price of $3,425, a wheelbase of 120 inches and a basic curb weight of 4,075 pounds minus passengers and gas. This 1941 Special was the choice of Fish Tail Ranch in Montana, but it prowled the Mountain West (below), rowboat presumably at the ready, looking for good trout streams.

[Left, below and overleaf: The 1941 Packard.]

1948 PACKARD

❁

While most of Detroit's car-makers waited for 1949 to unveil their completely revamped postwar designs, Packard chose to do so in 1948. Packard designers introduced their massive "flow-through" fender, which made their cars among the most distinctive on the road, certainly by comparison to the Fords and Chevrolets that maintained many elements of prewar styling. Detractors called the car a "pregnant elephant," but today the woodies of this vintage are considered classics. The lines of wood flow with the fender, creating a pleasing look. The 1948 Packard Station Sedan Wagon Model 2293 was powered by a 130-horsepower, 288 cubic inch straight eight-cylinder engine. It had an advertised list price of $3,425, a wheelbase of 120 inches and a basic curb weight of 4,075 pounds.

[*Left, below and overleaf: The 1948 Packard wagon.*]

1948
PLYMOUTH

The styling of the Plymouths of the immediate postwar years clearly had their roots in the designs which had been put on the road in 1940-1942. The grille was bolder in 1946-1948, and that reflected the general feeling of optimism that prevailed during those years. Other distinctive features were the redesigned hood ornament and the parking light molded into the chrome trim beneath the headlights. The amber fog lights seen in the example on these pages were not a stock item, however. The 1948 Plymouth P15C Special DeLuxe woodie wagon was powered by a 95-horsepower, 217.8 cubic inch straight six-cylinder engine. It had an advertised list price of $2,068. These cars had a wheelbase of 117 inches (common to Plymouth since 1940) and a basic curb weight of 3,320 pounds minus passengers and gas.

[*Below and right: A 1948 Super DeLuxe.*]

1 9 4 9
PLYMOUTH

As with most of Detroit, the Plymouth introduced its first all-new postwar styling in the 1949 model year. As with contemporary Chryslers and Dodges, the new look clearly reflected the philosophy of K.T. Keller, who took over the Chrysler Corporation when Walter Chrysler died in 1940. Keller was firmly opposed to the radical redesign mood that was then sweeping Detroit. He believed that cars should be made for people rather than for designers, and he was convinced that people wanted box-like utility. In 1949, that is what he delivered. The 1949 Plymouth P15C Special DeLuxe wagon was powered by a 95-horsepower, 217.8 cubic inch straight six-cylinder engine. It had an advertised list price of $2,068 new. These cars retained the 117inch wheelbase of earlier years and weighed 3,320 pounds.

[Left and below: A 1949 Chrysler Super DeLuxe wagon.]

1 9 5 0
P L Y M O U T H

For 1950, Plymouth offered a styling similar to 1949 – albeit with a redesigned grille – and a choice of three wagons. Two of these were two-door models, the P19 Deluxe Suburban and the P19 Deluxe Suburban Special. The third was the four-door P20 Special DeLuxe wagon. The most beautiful car that Plymouth would produce for 1950, it had structural wood, with finely crafted tongue-and-groove joints. The P19 was built on a 111 inch wheelbase, and the P20 on a 118.5-inch wheelbase. Each was powered by a 97-horsepower, 217.8 cubic inch straight six-cylinder engine. The basic curb weights of the trio were 3,116, 3,155 and 3,353 pounds respectively.The P19s were priced at $1,840 and $1,946 respectively and 34,457 were sold. The larger P20 woodie, priced at $2,372, sold only 2,057 units.

[*Below and right: Hugh and Marylou Forrest's 1950 P20.*]

1936-1939 PONTIACS

The evolution of Pontiac styling during the latter half of the 1930s was largely the result of an incredible team effort. Among those worth noting are Benjamin Anabel, chief of engineering for GM's Pontiac Division; Franklin Q. Hershey, the chief of design; designer Virgil Exner, who later had a brilliant career with Studebaker and Chrysler, and William Signius Knudsen. One of the greatest geniuses in the history of industrial production, Knudsen was trained by Henry Ford, headed Pontiac, served as president of GM from 1937 to 1940, and masterminded national industrial expansion during World War II. Hershey designed the graceful prow and wrapped it around Anabel's powerful straight eight-cylinder engine, while Exner deftly trimmed the cars in wood and chrome.

[Right: A 1939 DeLuxe with nonstandard hood ornament.]

[Below: A Pontiac woodie for 1936.]

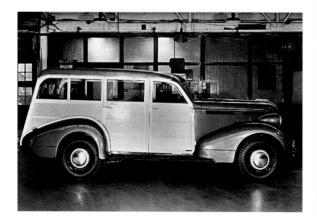

1 9 3 7
PONTIAC

◉

By the 1937 model year, Pontiac styling was defined by the design work of Franklin Q. Hershey and Virgil Exner. One of the most prominent features was the chrome trim that had prompted Pontiac to adopt the "Silver Streak" trademark for some of the cars in the line. In 1937, Pontiac produced two engines – the 100-horsepower, 248.9 straight eight-cylinder and the 85-horsepower, 222.7 cubic inch straight six-cylinder engine – but a woodie wagon was offered only with the straight six option. This was the 6CA DeLuxe Six wagon, which had an advertised list price of $992. The wheelbase was increased from 112 inches to 117 inches for 1937 for all the six cylinder Pontiacs, and among the nine models, 179,244 were sold. The 6CA DeLuxe woodie had a basic curb weight of 3,340 pounds.

[Below, right and overleaf: A 1937 Pontiac woodie wagon.]

1 9 3 8
P O N T I A C

✦

In 1938, with plenty of chrome for the era, and a bold new grille, Pontiac continued its promotion of what it called "New Silver Streak Beauty." It was not exactly new, for the Silver Streak concept had been around for several years. In 1938, as before, woodies continued to be a modest but important part of the line. The 6DA DeLuxe Six wagon for 1938 was powered by an 85-horsepower, 222.7 cubic inch straight six-cylinder engine. It had an advertised list price of $1,006 new, and between the eight six-cylinder models, 77,713 units were sold, though not all were woodies. These cars each had a wheelbase of 117 inches and the wagon had a basic curb weight of 3,530 pounds minus passengers and gas. In 1938, Pontiac also offered a 100-horsepower, 248.9 cubic inch straight eight-cylinder engine.

[*These pages and overleaf: Gary Woolery's straight eight '38.*]

1939·1940 PONTIACS

✳

I n the 1939 and 1940 model years, Pontiac reached the apogee of prewar styling, and became one of the top five Detroit car-makers. However, while companies such as Ford maintained their own wood mills, Pontiac was still outsourcing its woodwork from firms such as Hercules and Ionia. The 1939 Pontiac 6EA Quality DeLuxe wagon seen here was powered by an 85-horsepower, 222.7 cubic inch straight six-cylinder engine. It had an advertised list price of $990. The 1940 Pontiac 25HA Special Six wagon was powered by an 87-horsepower, 222.7 cubic inch straight six. It had an advertised list price of $1,015, and among the five models 106,892 were sold. The 6EA had a wheelbase of 115 inches while the 25HA's was 117 inches. The former weighed 3,175 pounds, while the 1940 woodie weighed 3,295 pounds.

[Left: Pontiac wood detail from 1939.]

[Below: Happy camping in a 1940 Pontiac woodie.]

1946
PONTIAC

✦

The first postwar Pontiacs were similar to prewar Pontiacs, but more chrome was added and rear fender guards were standard. The 1946 Pontiac 26LB Streamliner Six and 28LB Streamliner Eight wagons were powered by 90- or 103-horsepower, 239.2 or 248.9 cubic inch straight six-cylinder or straight eight engines. Advertised list price was $1,942 or $1,970 respectively. The two models had a generous wheelbase of 122 inches, and basic curb weights were 3,790 pounds and 3,870 pounds.

[*Above: A 1946 Pontiac Streamliner Eight.*]

[*Below, opposite and overleaf: Tom Templeton's 1946 Streamliner woodie.*]

1948
PONTIAC (I)

✦

For 1948, Pontiac styling was generally similar to that of the two preceding model years with the familiar chrome of the "Silver Streak" look. The big change was on the inside. General Motors' HydraMatic transmission, which had previously been been available in the Oldsmobile, was introduced as a Pontiac option. For an additional $185, Pontiac buyers could now experience one of the most important innovations in in the driving experience to come out of Detroit. Not to leave styling secondary to technology, Pontiac offered a DeLuxe trim option for $120 that included a potpourri of extras such as gravel guards, wheel discs and chrome fender moldings. These were more popular with the all-metal 1948 models, though. For woodie buyers, the wood itself was all the trim package they were seeking.

───────

[Left and below: A classic 1948 Pontiac woodie.]

1948
PONTIAC (II)

n 1948, Pontiac offered a choice of two Silver Streak woodie wagons: the Silver Streak Streamliner Six DeLuxe and the Silver Streak Streamliner Eight DeLuxe . The Streamliner Six was powered by a 90-horsepower, 239.2 cubic inch straight six-cylinder engine. It had an advertised list price of $2,442 with standard transmission, or $2,627 with the Hydramatic transmission option. The Streamliner Six had a wheelbase of 122 inches and a basic curb weight of 3,695 pounds minus passengers and gas. The Streamliner Eight DeLuxe wagon was powered by a 104-horsepower, 248.9 cubic inch straight eight-cylinder engine. It had an advertised list price of $2,490 with standard transmission or $2,695 with Hydramatic. The Streamliner Eight had a wheelbase of 122 inches and a basic curb weight of 3,765 pounds.

[These pages and overleaf: This woodie was a Silver Streak.]

POSTSCRIPT

Half a century has passed since the major carmakers produced woodies with real structural wood. From the mid-1950s to the present, they built numerous models with plastic and fiberglass simulated wood, but it is the *real* woodies that still turn heads and bring a smile. Woodies are special for many reasons – for the warmth of the wood, the nostalgia of a bygone era, and for the relaxed lifestyle that they evoke. With this in mind, what better postscript to this volume than to imagine taking off for the beach or mountains for a few days in a vehicle such as Cliff Parker's 1940 Ford DeLuxe, WZATREE, and its 1948 maple and mahogany teardrop trailer known as TREEHSE? With these, any coastside or mountain campground is a suitable place to stop for a night or two, or maybe three.

[*Left and below: WZATREE and companion TREEHSE.*]

INDEX

✦

[Overleaf: A detail from Brent and Tobi

Allred's 1948 Mercury known as REDWOOD.]

[Last page: "Beach wood" says it all.]

IT'S NOT JUST A WOODIE

CALIFORNIA

BECHWUD

IT'S AN ATTITUDE